# Spectacular Spots

Written and Illustrated by
Susan Stockdale

PEACHTREE
ATLANTA

For Todd, always

Published by
PEACHTREE PUBLISHING COMPANY INC.
1700 Chattahoochee Avenue
Atlanta, Georgia 30318-2112
*PeachtreeBooks.com*


First trade paperback edition published in 2022
First bilingual edition published in 2017



Art direction by Loraine Joyner
Typesetting by Melanie McMahon Ives

The illustrations were created in acrylic on paper.

On the front cover: leatherback turtle
On the back cover: Helmeted Guineafowl

Printed in February 2022 by Toppan Leefung in China

10 9 8 7 6 5 4 3 2 1 (hardcover)
10 9 8 7 6 5 4 3 2 1 (trade paperback)
HC ISBN: 978-1-56145-817-2
PB ISBN: 978-1-68263-396-0

Also available in bilingual edition
PB ISBN: 978-1-56145-978-0
BB ISBN: 978-1-68263-368-7

Cataloging-in-Publication Data is available from the Library of Congress.

Spots on creatures all around,

way up high

and on the ground.

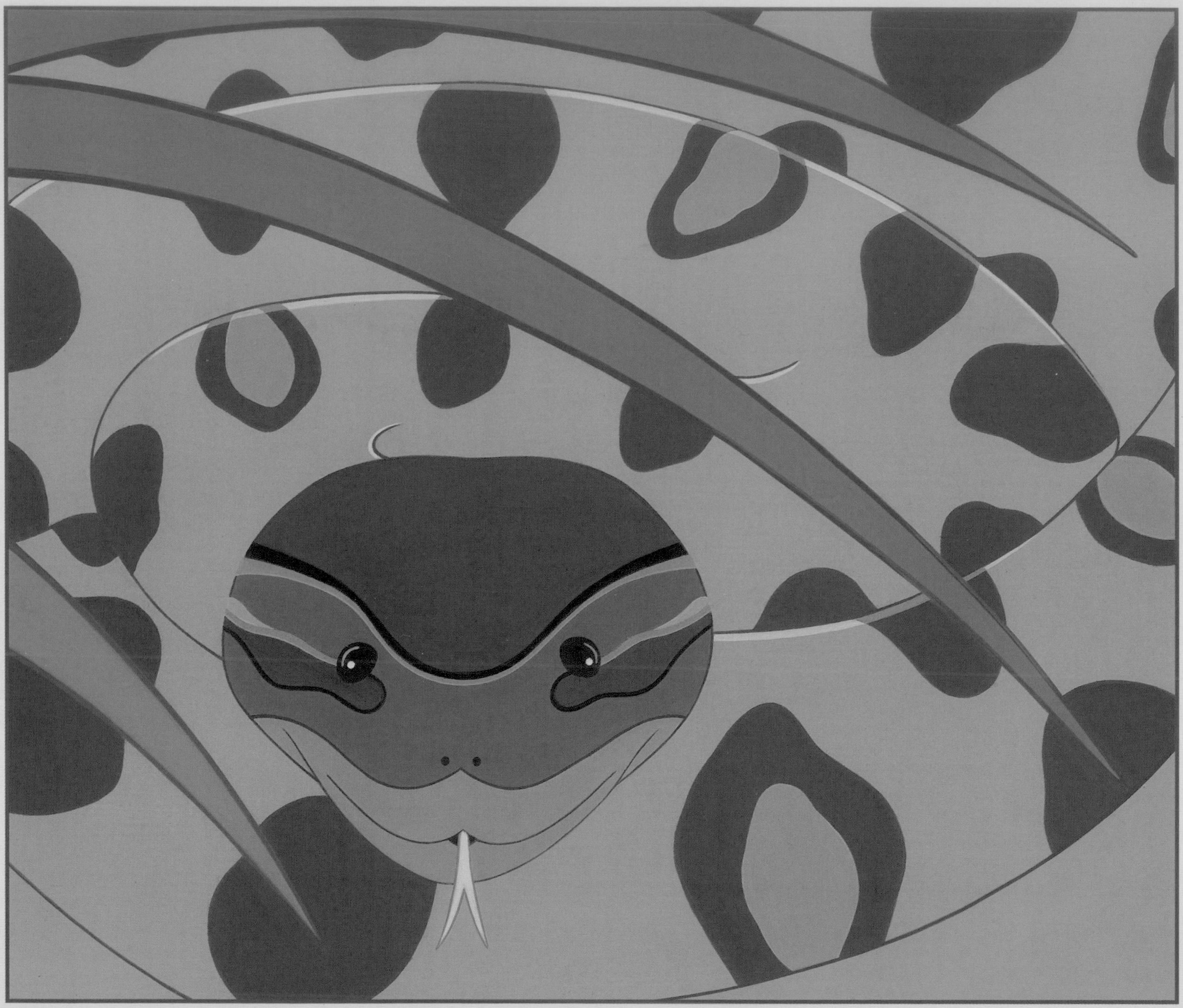

Spots on snakes

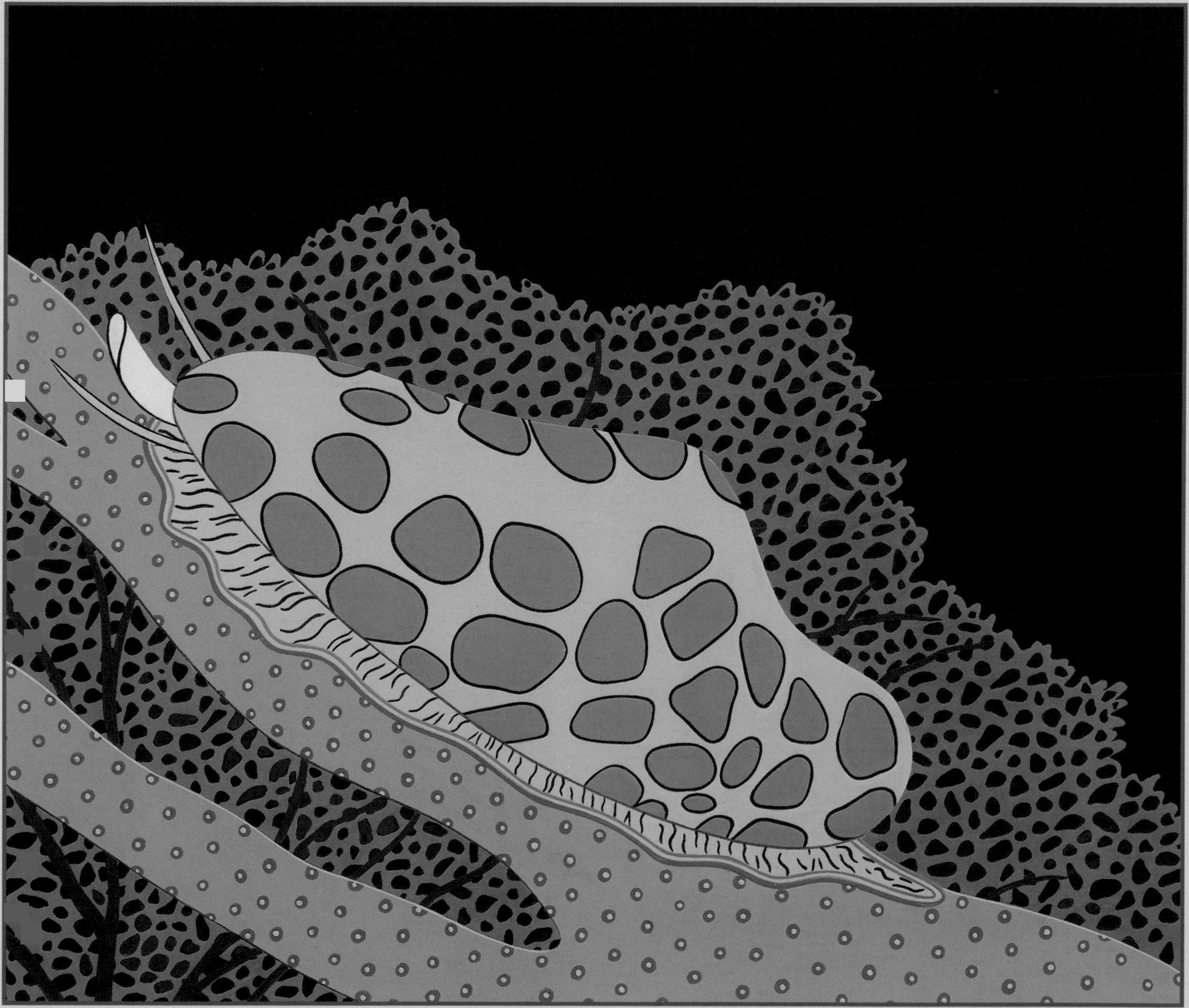

and gliding snails.

Swimming turtles,

singing quails.

Crawling crabs

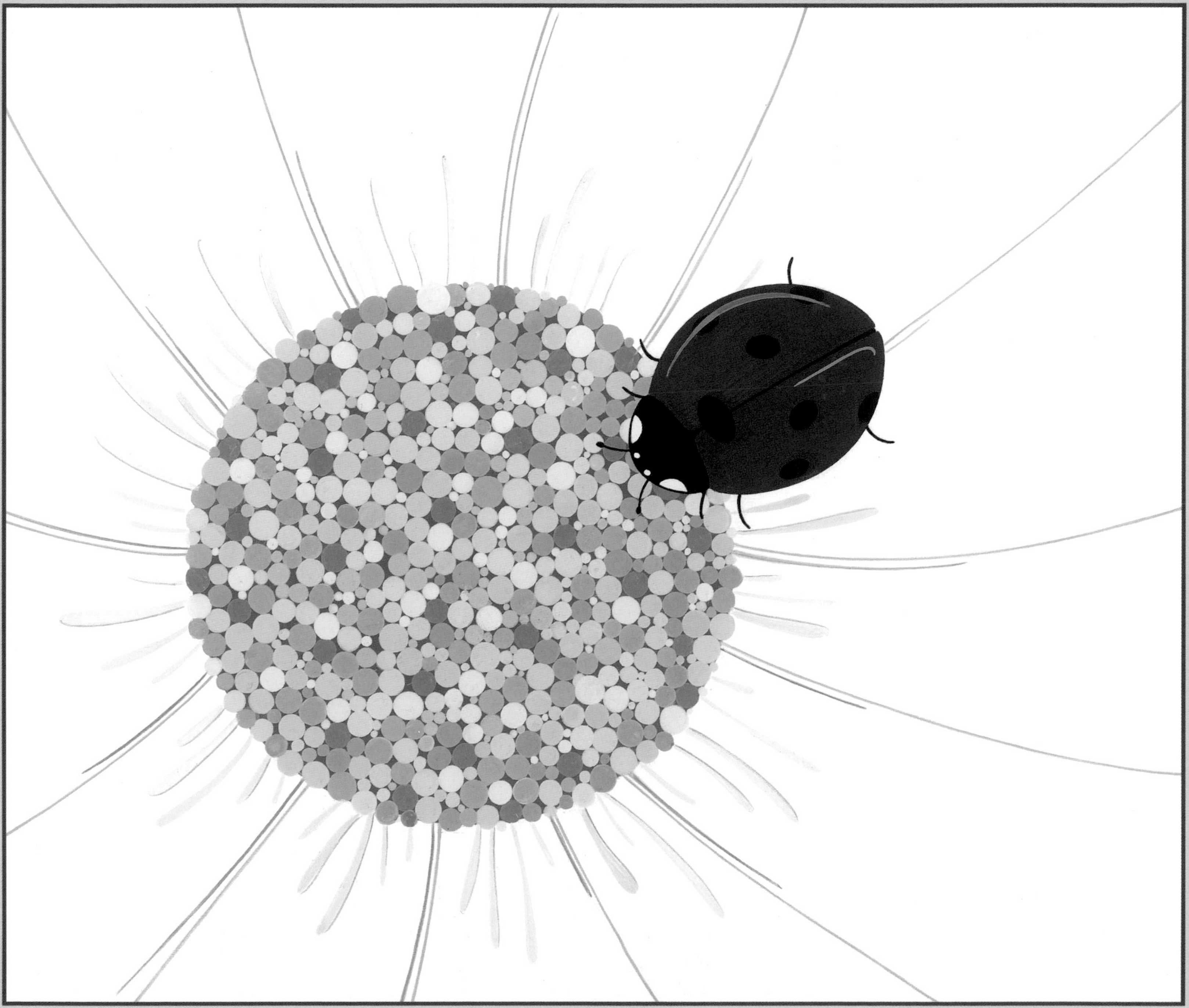

and munching bugs.

Charging cheetahs,

creeping slugs.

Dashing horses,

dozing hogs.

Scouting fish

and clinging frogs.

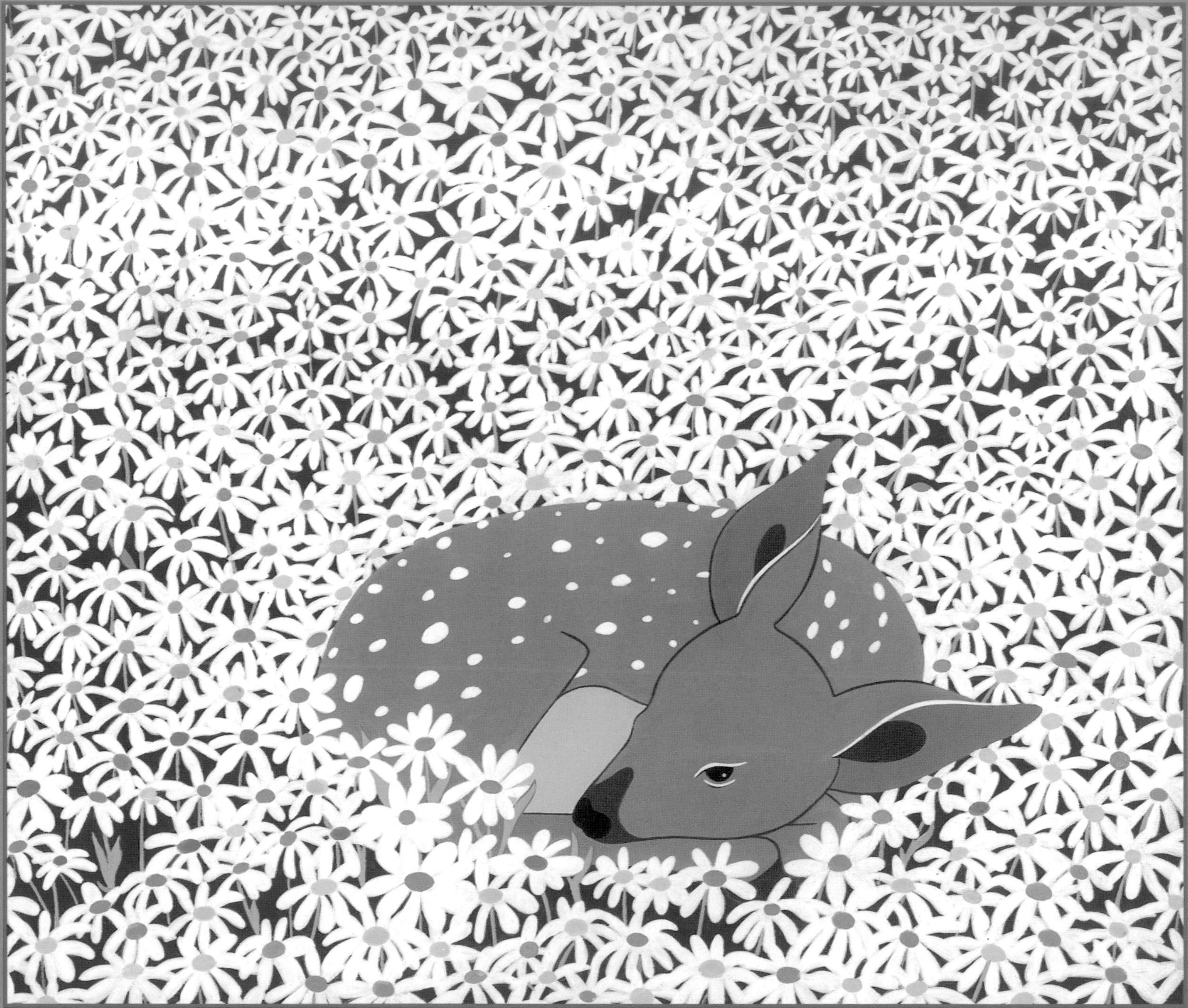

Napping fawn

and strutting fowl.

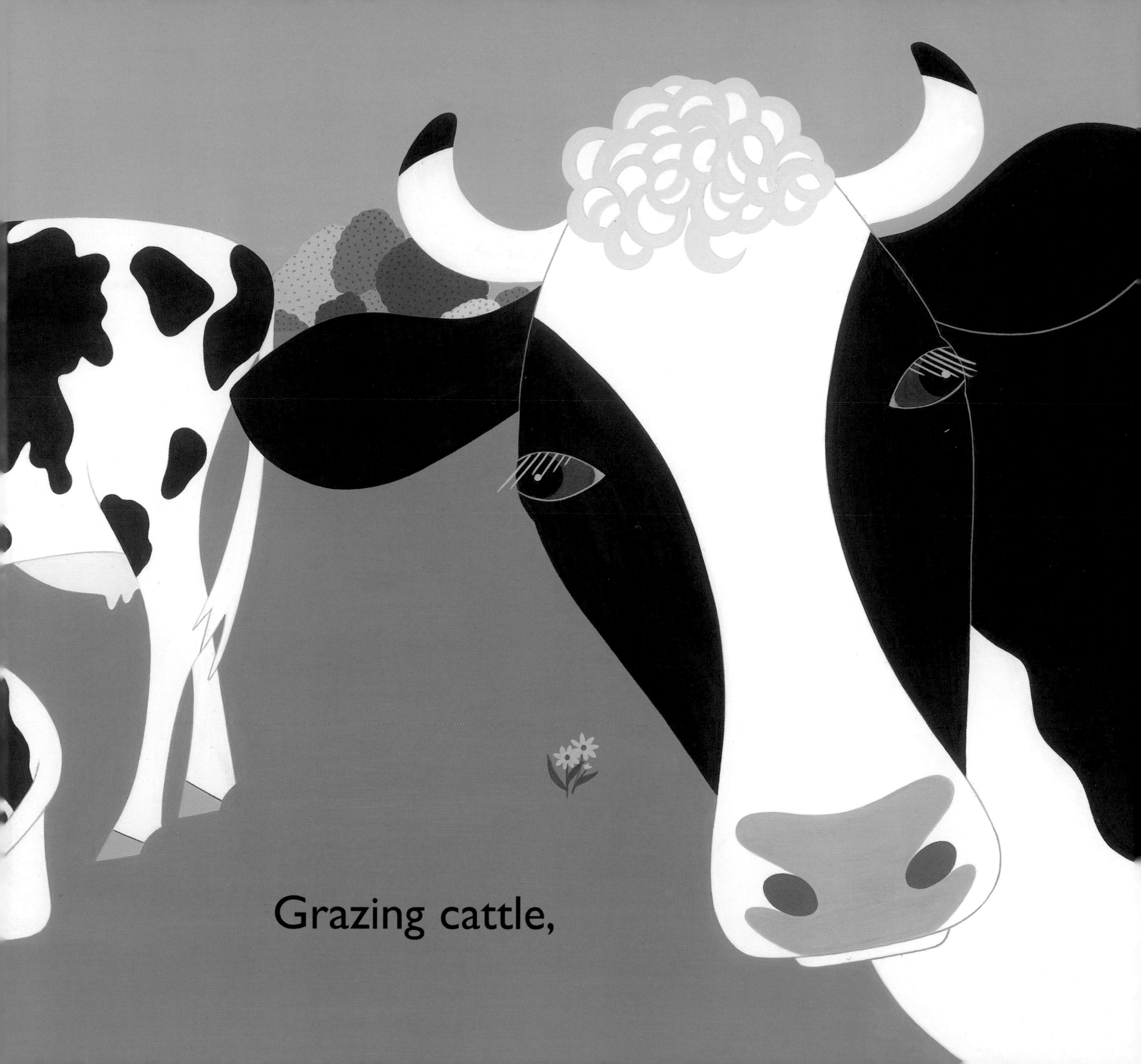

Grazing cattle,

swooping owl.

Spots with purpose, spots with flair.

Spotted creatures everywhere!

"Eyespots" on a **buckeye butterfly** mimic the eyes of a larger creature, scaring off predators that might want to eat it. (Caribbean, Mexico, and the southernmost parts of the United States; insect)

The **jaguar** and the **spotted ground squirrel** blend in with their surroundings as a result of their spots. (Jaguar: southwestern United States to South America; mammal; spotted ground squirrel: Canada to Mexico; mammal)

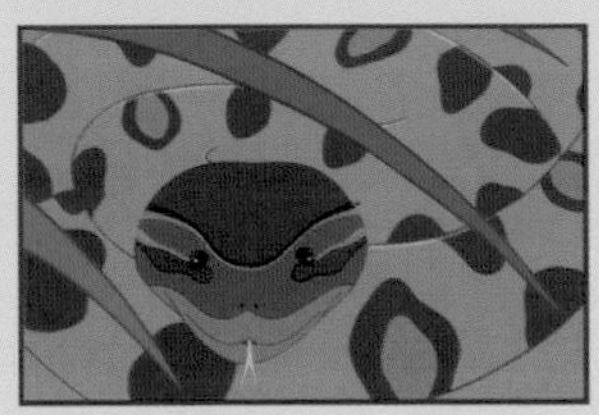

Dark green spots on the **green anaconda** help hide it in the leafy jungle. Green anacondas are the heaviest snakes in the world, weighing up to 550 pounds (250 kg). (South America; reptile)

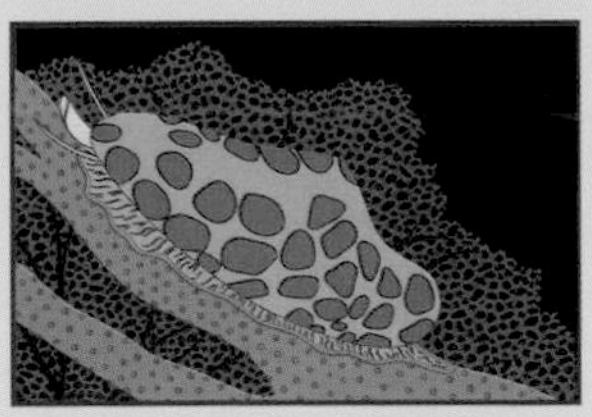

Predators are warned away by the colorfully patterned shell of the **flamingo tongue snail.** It feeds on poisonous sea coral, becoming toxic itself but remaining unharmed. (Tropical waters of the western Atlantic Ocean, including the Caribbean Sea; mollusk)

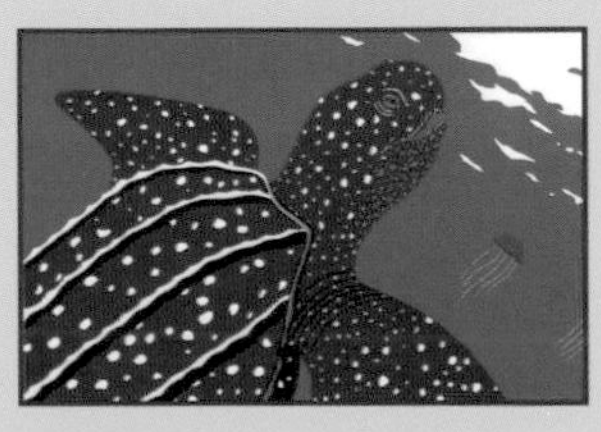

The dappled black shell of the **leatherback turtle** blends well with the dark waters of the open ocean. Leatherbacks are the largest of all living turtles. (All tropical and subtropical oceans, extending into the Arctic Circle; reptile)

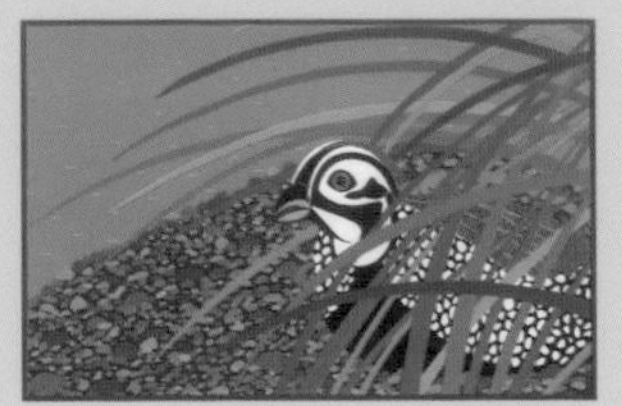

The male **Montezuma Quail** sings nine descending notes in a whinnying call to attract a mate. Its patterned feathers help this ground-dwelling bird avoid detection by predators. (Mexico and southwestern United States; bird)

Camouflaged by its patterned shell, the **calico crab** buries itself in the sand. It darts out of its hiding place to seize prey with its sharp claws. (Western Atlantic Ocean from the Chesapeake Bay to the Dominican Republic; crustacean)

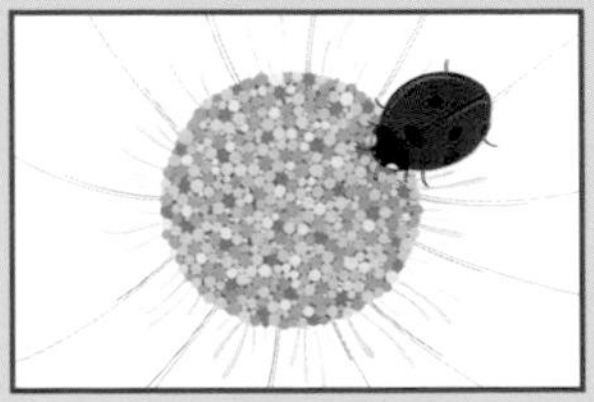

As the **ladybug** feeds on pollen and small insects found on plants, its bright coloring and spots warn enemies away. If disturbed, it emits a bad-smelling fluid. (All parts of the world except Antarctica; insect)

The **cheetah** is camouflaged by its spotted coat as it stalks prey in the tall grasses. It is the fastest land mammal, reaching speeds of up to 75 miles (120 km) per hour in short bursts. (Africa and Asia; mammal)

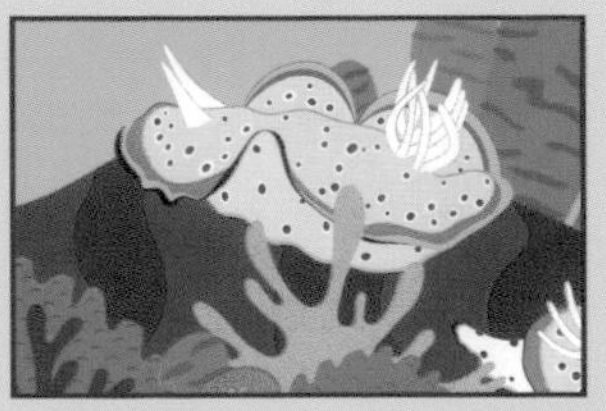

Also known as a sea slug, the **nudibranch** often gets its brilliant coloring from the coral, sponges, and anemones it eats. Its colors may warn predators that it is poisonous. (Oceans worldwide; mollusk)

**Appaloosa horse** develops a spotted pattern. The coloring and spotting on each horse is unique. Like our fingerprints, no two patterns are exactly alike! (North America; mammal)

The color and size of spots on the **hog** vary a great deal. Also known as a pig, it is a very intelligent animal with a keen sense of smell. (All continents except Antarctica; mammal)

Vivid colors on the **blue boxfish** may signal to other ocean animals that it is deadly to eat. The fish needs this protection because it is a very slow swimmer. (Indian and Pacific oceans; fish)

Bright colors and bold spots on the **blue poison dart frog** warn rainforest creatures of its toxic nature. Some poison dart frogs are considered the most poisonous animals in the world. (South America; amphibian)

It can be hard for predators to find the **white-tailed deer fawn**; its spotted coat blends in with its surroundings. The spots disappear when the fawn matures. (Canada to South America; mammal)

The spotted feathers of the **Helmeted Guineafowl** are often used by people to decorate jewelry, hair ornaments, and other products. The male bird attacks other males who try to take his mate by ramming them with the bony "helmet" on his head. (Native to Africa but widely introduced elsewhere; bird)

Known for its distinctive black and white markings, the average **Holstein cow** produces about 23,000 pounds (10,400 kg) of milk each year! Many products such as cheese, butter, and ice cream are made from milk. (All continents except Antarctica; mammal)

The **Spotted Owl** glides silently down to grab small mammals like flying squirrels and woodrats with its talons. Then it kills its prey with its sharp beak, often eating it whole. (United States and Canada; bird)

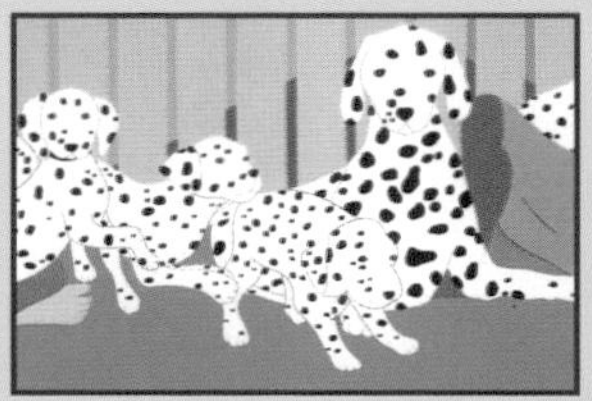

**Dalmatian** puppies are born completely white and develop spots as they age. A popular companion and pet, the Dalmatian is also used as a rescue dog. (All continents except Antarctica; mammal)

# Can you find the animals that belong to these SPOTS?

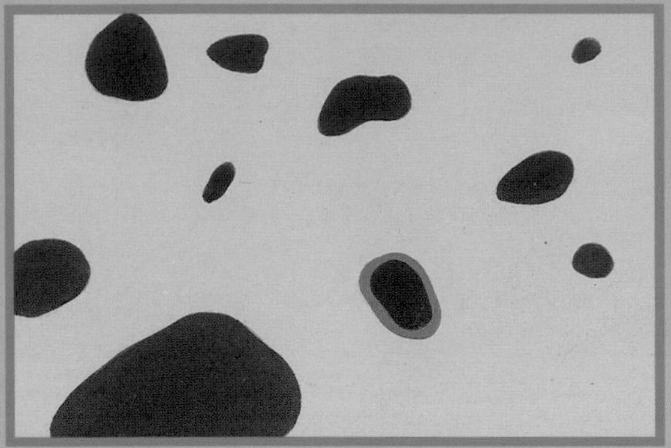
Appaloosa horse

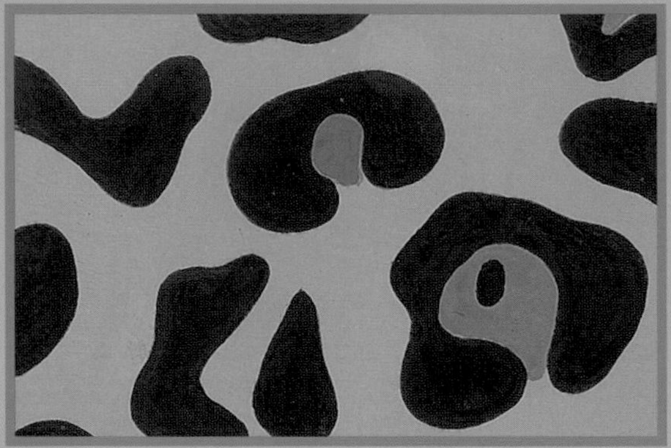
jaguar

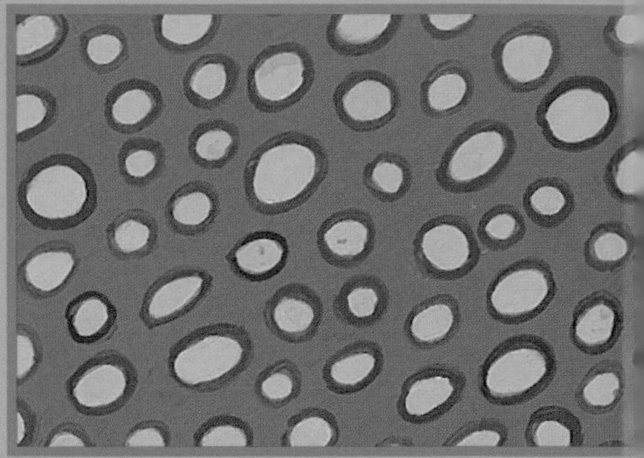
Spotted Owl

Montezuma Quail

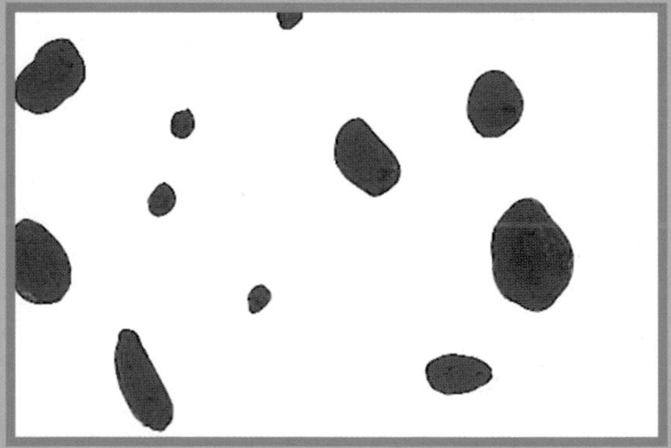
Dalmatian

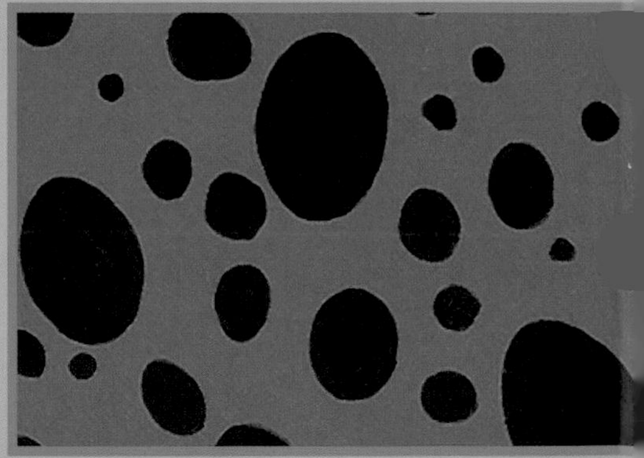
blue poison dart frog

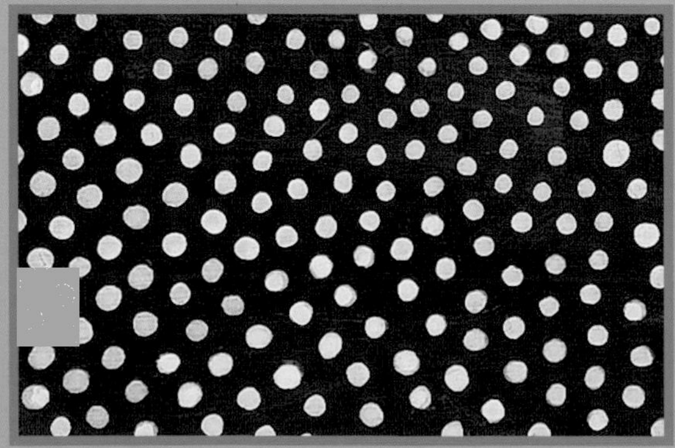
Helmeted Guineafowl

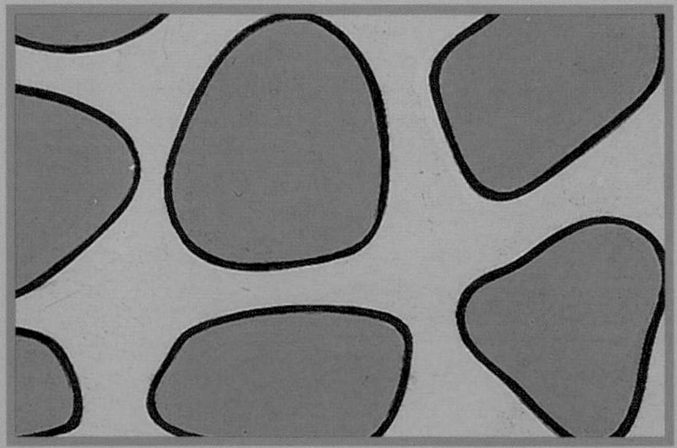
flamingo tongue snail

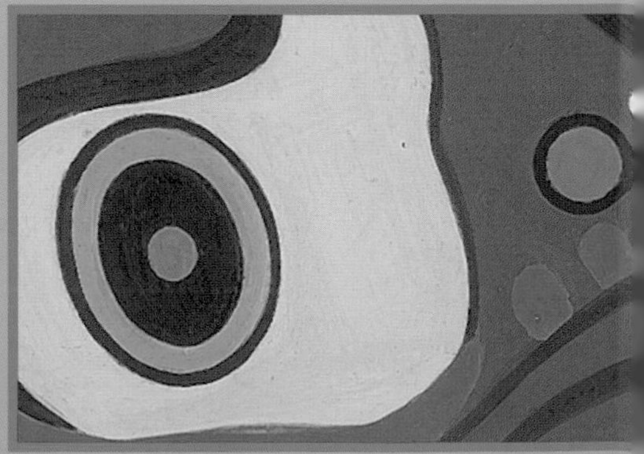
buckeye butterfly

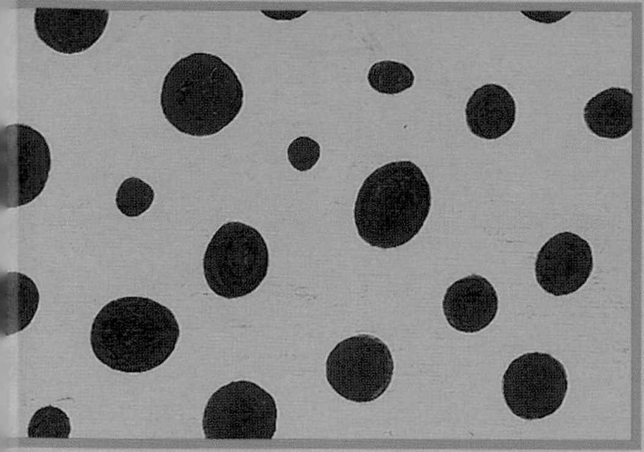
chee

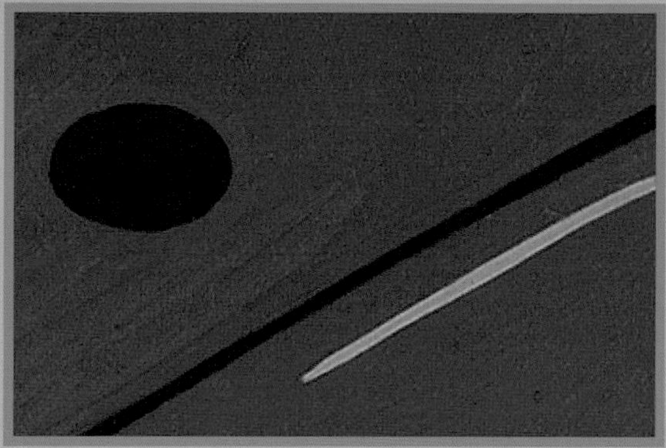
ladybug

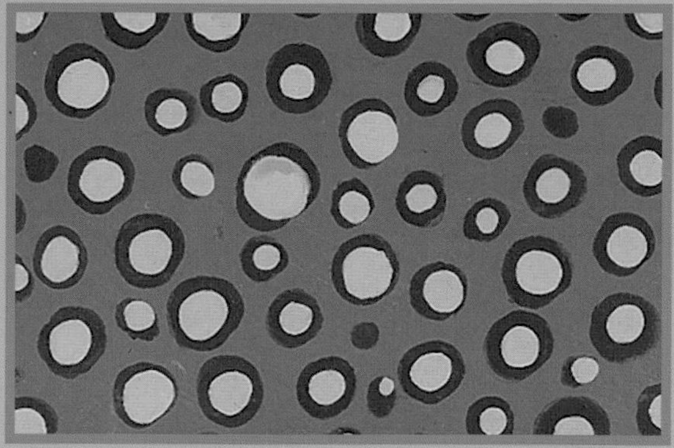
blue boxfish

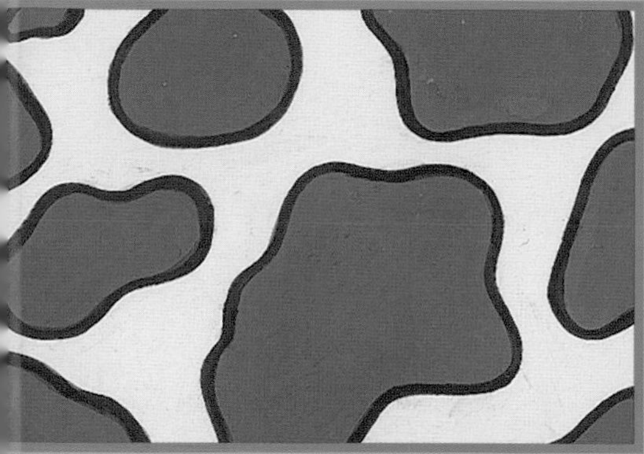
calico c

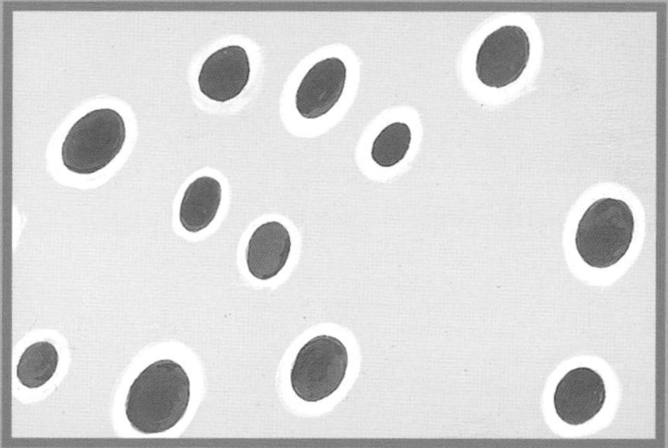
nudibranch

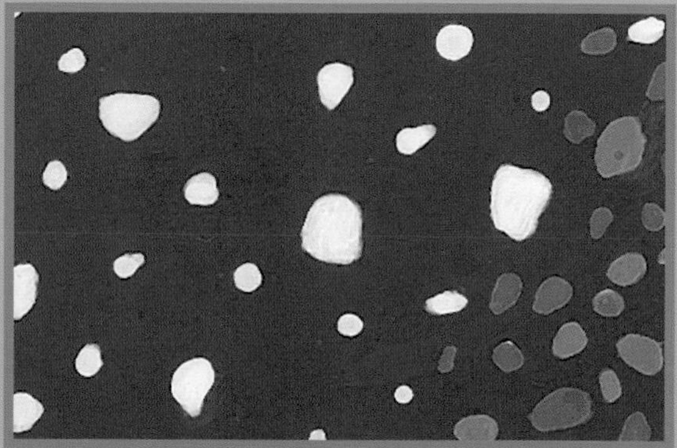
leatherback turtle

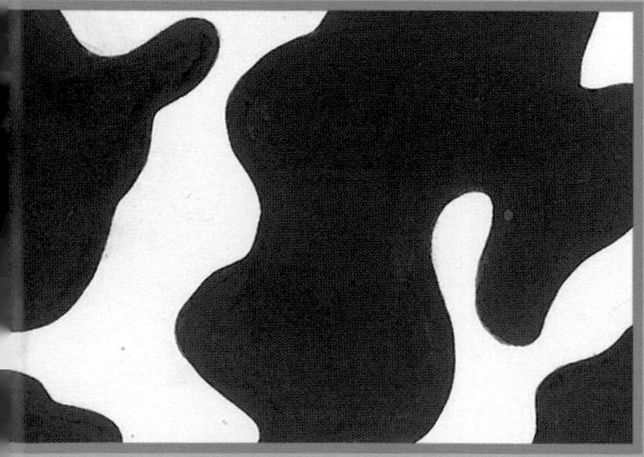
Holstein c

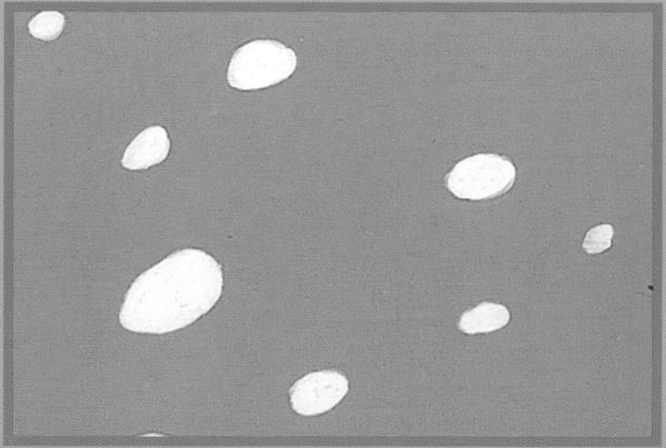
white-tailed deer fawn

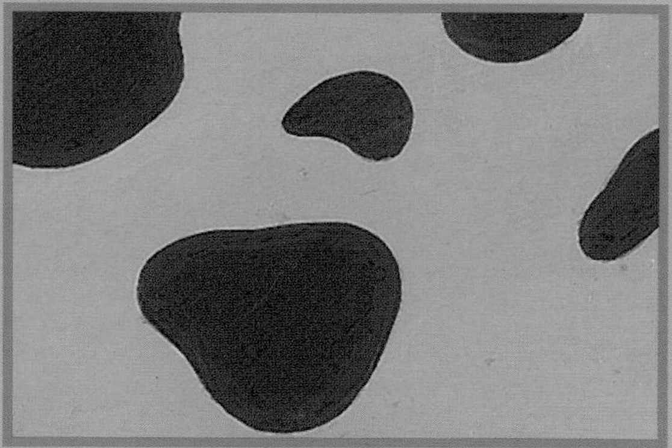
hog

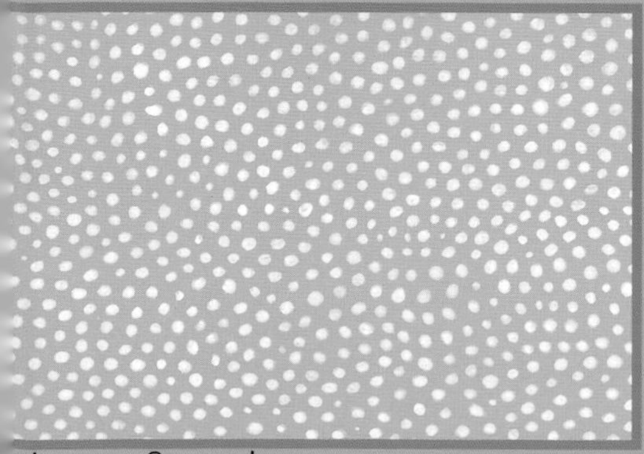
spotted ground squ

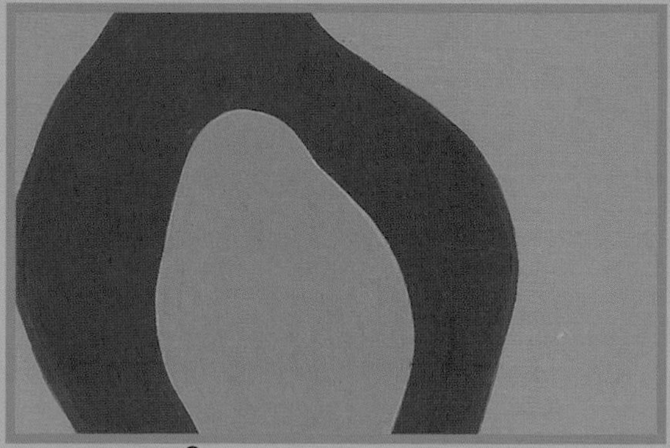
green anaconda

Turn the book upside down to read the correct answers.

I am grateful to many scientists for their research assistance. They include Dr. Kevin de Queiroz, Dr. Carla Dove, Dr. Jerry Harasewych, Dr. Kristofer Helgen, Dr. Robert Hershler, Mr. Gary F. Hevel, Dr. Dave Johnson, Dr. Victor G. Springer, and Dr. Ellen Strong, all with the Smithsonian Institution's National Museum of Natural History, and Dr. Natalia J. Vandenberg of the U.S. Department of Agriculture. I thank them all for helping me bring SPECTACULAR SPOTS to life.